# ALLEN IVERSON

## NEVER GIVE UP

*Titles in the* **SPORTS LEADERS** *Series:*

## Vince Carter
0-7660-2173-4

## Allen Iverson
0-7660-2174-2

## Derek Jeter
0-7660-2035-5

## Jason Kidd
0-7660-2214-5

## Shaquille O'Neal
0-7660-2175-0

# ALLEN IVERSON

## NEVER GIVE UP

John Albert Torres

**Enslow Publishers, Inc.**

40 Industrial Road
Box 398
Berkeley Heights, NJ 07922
USA

PO Box 38
Aldershot
Hants GU12 6BP
UK

http://www.enslow.com

**Library of Congress Cataloging-in-Publication Data**

Torres, John Albert.
    Allen Iverson : never give up / John Albert Torres.— 1st ed.
        p. cm. — (Sports leaders series)
    Summary: Discusses the personal life and basketball career of the star guard for the Philadelphia 76ers, Allen Iverson.
    Includes bibliographical references and index.
        ISBN 0-7660-2174-2
        1. Iverson, Allen, 1975– —Juvenile literature. 2. Basketball players—United States—Biography—Juvenile literature. [1. Iverson, Allen, 1975– 2. Basketball players. 3. African Americans—Biography.]
    I. Title. II. Series.
    GV884.I84T67 2004
    796.323'092—dc22
                                                    2003015334

Printed in the United States of America

10 9 8 7 6 5 4 3 2

**Illustration Credits:** Al Bello/Getty Images, pp. 52, 55; Doug Pensinger/ALLSPORT, pp. 46, 57; Doug Pensinger/Getty Images, pp. 29, 82, 88; Ezra Shaw/ALLSPORT, pp. 20, 31; Ezra Shaw/Getty Images, pp. 22, 62; Glenn James/NBAE/Getty Images, p. 26; Jamie Squire/Getty Images, p. 48; Jason Wise/Getty Images, p. 69; Jed Jacobsohn/ALLSPORT, pp. 12, 17; Jeff Reinking/NBAE/Getty Images, p. 6; Jonathan Daniel/ALLSPORT, pp. 66, 90; Jonathan Ferrey/Getty Images, p. 34; Ken Regan/NBAE/Getty Images, p. 71; M. David Leeds/ALLSPORT/Getty Images, p. 86; Matthew Stockman/Getty Images, p. 59; Noren Trotman/NBAE via Getty Images, p. 36; Otto Greule, Jr./ALLSPORT, pp. 9, 11, 14, 45; Tom Pidgeon/Getty Images, pp. 41, 76.

**Cover Illustration:** Jeff Reinking/NBAE/Getty Images.

# CONTENTS

# GREATEST GAME

It had been a great game, and the crowd had been cheering for the better part of three hours. In fact, it had been a better game than most people expected. The Philadelphia 76ers had really given the Los Angeles Lakers a run for their money in the first game of the 2001 NBA Finals. Many people did not think Philadelphia would even be able to win one game in the series, but the 76ers managed to force the opening game into overtime. That's when Shaquille O'Neal and Kobe Bryant combined for five quick points to give the Lakers a 99–94 lead with less than three minutes left. It looked like it would be the outcome most people had expected.

The Los Angeles crowd filling the Staples Center was already celebrating. After all, all the experts had predicted the Lakers would sweep their way to a second consecutive league title. They had not lost a game since the beginning of April, winning 19 consecutive games including an incredible 11 in the playoffs. Some were calling them unbeatable. Earlier in the game fans had chanted "sweep, sweep," as the hometown favorites scored 16 straight points for an early 18–5 lead. Sure, the games still had to be played, but not many people believed in the Sixers. But the Sixers, led by Allen Iverson, believed in themselves. Iverson's hot hand in the first half caused the "sweep" chants to stop. Fans began "oohing and aahing" as Iverson dazzled the crowd and the Lakers with a series of dunks, lay-ups, jump shots, and of course, his crossover dribble. He tantalized the crowd and toyed with defenders, as he seemed to be able to score at will. Iverson did not celebrate or trash talk as much as normal. He seemed to be more serious, more determined to show the world his team belonged on this big stage.

After Philadelphia's Raja Bell flung up a desperation shot in overtime that somehow went through as the 24-second shot clock expired, the Sixers were only down three. The defense tightened up and held

Allen Iverson exchanges words with Kobe Bryant of the Los Angeles Lakers during a brief break in the action during the 2001 NBA Finals.

the Lakers without a basket. That is when Iverson took over. He drove down the right side of the lane and somehow was able to get good position to draw a foul. Iverson, the man nicknamed "The Answer," calmly sank two free throws to make it a 99–98 game.

The crowd had stopped celebrating and there seemed to be a shocked silence throughout the arena. Now many of the Lakers faithful were looking at the clock, hoping it would move a little faster and give the Lakers the win. But there was still 1:46 left in the game when Tyronn Lue missed an ill-advised drive for the Lakers. Iverson took the loose ball and beat everyone down court. He had a clear path to the basket and a slam-dunk would have given Philadelphia a one-point lead. Instead, Iverson raced to the left side of the top of the key, lined up in three-point territory and sank the trey to give the Sixers a two-point lead.

> Iverson dazzled the crowd and the Lakers with a series of dunks, lay-ups, jump shots, and of course, his crossover dribble.

Most players would have settled for the easy basket. But Iverson smelled a victory, and he did not hesitate to go for the long jumper. His confidence

*Allen Iverson hoists a clutch three-pointer during the 2001 NBA Finals.*

*Iverson celebrates after hitting a big three-point shot against the Lakers in Game 1 of the 2001 NBA Finals.*

was enough to enable him to go for the big shot—the one that just might finish the Lakers. Once the ball made its way through the white net, the momentum instantly went to Philadelphia.

"That's the way we are," Iverson would say later. "We play hard and we came in here expecting to win."[1]

Laker Rick Fox turned the ball over on Los Angeles' next possession, and the Sixers knew who to get the ball to. Point guard Eric Snow waited patiently for Iverson to work his way through a few picks before getting him the ball in the right corner. Iverson did not hesitate; he had the answer, another two points. Iverson pounded his chest as he ran back down court. He had scored seven straight points at the end of overtime! The crowd was stunned and their silence filled the arena.

The teams traded baskets and the Sixers held on to take the first game of the series, 107–101.

"Everyone said we can't do it, and that drives us," Iverson said. "We know we can win. Everybody's been counting us out."[2]

In all, Iverson finished with a game-high 48 points, an amazing total in any NBA game, but even more impressive in the NBA Finals. He single-handedly kept Philadelphia in the game early on

*Allen Iverson maneuvers through a crowd of Laker defenders in Game 1 of the 2001 NBA Finals.*

when he scored an amazing 30 points in the first half. During one segment, Iverson had two shots in a row blocked by Kobe Bryant, but he would not give up. He maneuvered around Kobe and hit a long jump shot from the corner as the shot clock was winding down. Kobe could do nothing but shake his head. Nobody could play better defense than Kobe just had, and still Iverson was able to score. Determination.

In the second half, the Lakers inserted the seldom-used Tyronn Lue to slow down Iverson, and he had some success. But the game belonged to "The Answer." Lue, a defensive specialist with lightning quick speed, said that it was tough guarding Iverson because of his wide array of offensive moves. He also said that Iverson is one of those rare players who go immediately into attack mode when he touches the ball. He said Iverson goes right after the defense on every play, never letting up on the pressure. The tactic he decided to try was to deny Iverson the ball, or at least make him work harder before he caught a pass. But that type of defense is almost impossible to perfect. Iverson would get his hands on the ball; there was no denying him.

Halfway through the third quarter, Iverson stole an errant pass meant for Shaquille O'Neal in the low post. He raced down court for a fast-break lay-up to give the Sixers a 68–56 lead. A few minutes later teammate Eric Snow made a three-point play and suddenly it looked as if the Sixers would run away with it. But the Lakers showed why they were the defending champs. They refused to give up and they came back strong. The score went back and forth for the rest of the game before going into overtime.

Iverson played 52 minutes in the contest and later collapsed in front of his locker after celebrating with his teammates. But he knew there was still work to do. Even though Allen Iverson, "The Answer," has had other games where he scored more than 48 points, Game 1 of the 2001 NBA Finals must rank as the greatest game he has ever played.

He played well throughout the rest of the series, but the Lakers were just too much for the cagey Philadelphia 76ers and took the next four games, winning their second consecutive title in a five-game series. After the buzzer sounded for the end of the fifth game, Iverson simply walked off the court and toward his locker room. Some people criticized the talented but controversial superstar, saying that he acted like a sore loser. But Iverson said that he simply

Allen Iverson blows past Lakers' center Shaquille O'Neal in Game 1 of the 2001 NBA Finals.

did not want to get in the way of the Lakers' celebration.

Another controversy had found Allen Iverson, arguably one of the greatest offensive players in the National Basketball Association. Even before Iverson entered the league as a highly heralded player with just two years of college under his belt, he had his share of critics lined up ready to take aim. And Iverson has done little to stay out of the spotlight. He has made as much news by his actions away from the basketball court as he has by his play on the hardwood.

Iverson's problems—ranging from an arrest while in high school, run-ins with his coaches, tardiness at practice, and even a controversial rap album—were well documented. His penchant for trouble even caused the 76ers to consider trading him. But how could you trade Allen Iverson, one of the top five players in the league, and expect to get equal value in return? Philadelphia's fans would never stand for it.

But equally impressive is the story of a fatherless child who overcame a poverty-filled childhood. He then overcame one obstacle after another to make it as one of the best high school and then college basketball players. Equally impressive is a young man who is fiercely loyal to his family and friends—so much so that even in his first year he resisted efforts by the 76ers and the NBA to keep him away from friends who some saw as being bad influences.

"The NBA can't pick my friends," he said. "When I was struggling growing up, no running water in my house, the electric lights turned off, these were the guys who were with me. They grew up with me. I'm not gonna turn my back on them now. Not many people were always angels as they grew up. These are the guys who won't always be telling me how great I am. They know me."[3]

As sure as the basketball is round, you can be sure Allen Iverson is going to do things in his own way. And why not? That is how he has always done things, and look where it has gotten him. He is one of the most recognizable players in the game of basketball today.

> "Everyone said we can't do it, and that drives us. We know we can win."
>
> —Allen Iverson

Iverson has come a long way from some of the worst drug-ridden poverty in America, has weathered one controversy after another, to make it as one of the formidable forces of the NBA and to put on a 48-point performance in Game 1 of the 2001 NBA Finals.

*Iverson looks to pass over the outstretched arm of the Lakers' Derek Fisher during Game 3 of the 2001 NBA Finals in Philadelphia.*

Today, the man they call "The Answer" has millions of children practicing his famous crossover dribble and fearless drives through defenders on his way to the basket. Without a doubt, Allen Iverson will continue to excite fans and critics for years to come as he creates his own path through NBA stardom. And one thing is for sure: He will do it his way.

# 2

# BUBBA CHUCK

Allen Ezail Iverson was born into extreme poverty on June 7, 1975, in Hampton, Virginia. It seemed as if right from the start Allen would have to start out with a lot less than most other children.

His biological father, Allen Broughton, never played a role in Allen's life and has been in and out of prisons since before Allen Iverson was born. Allen's maternal grandmother, the steadiest influence in the Iverson family, passed away shortly after Allen's birth. It was left to Ann, Allen's fifteen-year-old single mother, and her aging grandmother (Allen's great-grandmother) to raise him in one of Virginia's toughest neighborhoods.

The family's housing project apartment sat right atop some of the city's sewer lines. On more than one occasion the sewer lines broke and the family's apartment was flooded. The family got used to wearing shoes at all times just in case the floors were covered with raw sewage. Even today Iverson talks about and remembers the horrible smell throughout the home from the sewage lines.

Allen's mother, Ann, tried her hand at all sorts of jobs to help the family make ends meet. She worked as a secretary at Langley Air Force Base, a counter person in a convenience store, a welder in a shipyard, a forklift driver, and an Amway saleswoman. Still, the family often had their electricity and water turned off because she could not afford to pay the bills. They were also evicted from apartments several times. Life was tough.

Sometimes the only thing that got Ann through it all was the joy of her life, her son Allen, who she nicknamed Bubba Chuck. When Allen was born, two of his uncles came to visit him in the hospital. One was nicknamed Bubba and the other Chuck. They both asked Ann to nickname her new son after them. So she nicknamed Allen after both of them: Bubba Chuck.

"When Bubba Chuck was three, I told him,

'you're the man of the house. You gotta do whatever you gotta do to become a man,'" Ann said. Having a child at such a young age was a challenge that Ann had to face. Despite her young age she knew that she could not let her son down. "I'd wake up at night and feel Allen's chest, make sure his heart was still beating, and think, dag, this is my baby. He's relying on me. If I don't do right, he won't do right."[1]

That is how things were for the Iverson family—nothing was ever easy. When Allen was still a young boy, Ann moved in with boyfriend Michael Freeman. He fathered Allen's two sisters—Brandy, who was born in 1979, and Liesha, born in 1991.

From a very young age, Allen was athletic and loved to participate in sports. In youth baseball he was always the pitcher; in pickup football games with his friends he always played the quarterback; and in basketball he was the star scorer. But it was football that Allen really loved to play. It was on the football field that he was able to forget the poverty he faced every day at home.

> "When Bubba Chuck was three, I told him, 'you're the man of the house. . . . do whatever you gotta do to become a man."
> —Ann Iverson

*Allen Iverson's mother, Ann, cheers him on during a game against the Dallas Mavericks in Dallas on November 10, 2001.*

Melvin Stephens, Allen's lifelong friend, said that Allen was a great athlete even at Aberdeen Elementary School when the two were just boys. Stephens said that Allen was one of those kids you knew would make something of himself. The two were inseparable playing football and baseball all the time after school.

Freeman, who worked as a welder at the local shipyard, started teaching Allen to play basketball at a very young age. Allen was a naturally gifted athlete and took to the game immediately, showing great balance and ball-handling skills. There was only one thing that kept Allen from playing a lot of basketball as a kid: He did not want to.

Allen complained that the game was too soft and that there was not enough physical contact to hold his interest. When Freeman heard Allen's complaints, the boy's stepfather literally dragged Allen from the house to the local playground so Allen could watch and then participate in some pickup basketball games. Allen loved it. He was knocked down over and over again. But he kept getting up and continuing to play. The tougher the game was, the better Allen played. That was when he started to love the game.

It was on those playgrounds that Allen created

his now famous crossover dribble. He liked dribbling and faking out opponents almost as he much as he loved shooting and scoring. It was common for Allen to come home from the courts with scrapes and cuts and bruises. It almost seemed as if the harder the games got then the better he would play and the more he would enjoy the game. There was a determination in him every time he walked onto the court.

Somehow, Allen knew that someday he would be rich and be able to take his mother away from the poverty and the projects. He was not sure if it would be as a basketball player or a football player, but Allen always knew he would be someone big.

Like most kids his age, when Allen was a boy he would tell his mother every night that he was going to be rich one day and buy her a big house and a Jaguar convertible to drive around. He wanted to pay his mother back for all the love and support she gave him.

It was Allen's mother who sometimes would toughen him up for the challenges of life. She never hid any of the poverty from him, always letting him know why they were getting evicted or why the power had been shut off again. She also toughened him up when it came to playing sports. Sometimes

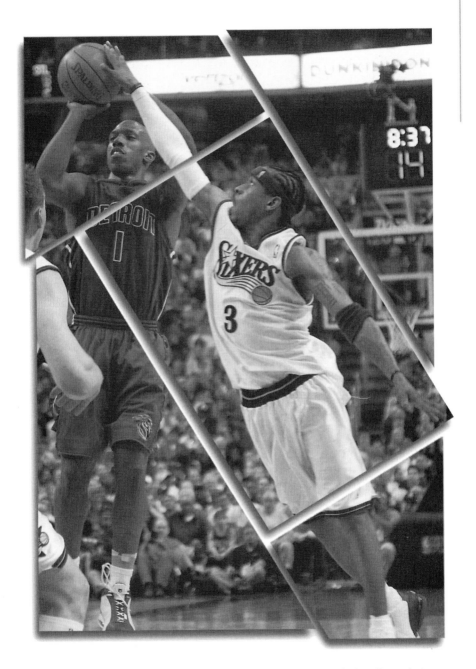

*Iverson blocks the shot of Chauncey Billups of the Detroit Pistons during a playoff game in May 2003.*

Allen would play football in his great-grandmother's backyard with his friends who were all bigger than he was. Sometimes they would play very rough and Allen would run into the house crying. But his mother, Ann, would send him right back out to continue playing. She would never let him quit. Ann knew that to survive in life, Allen would have to have the toughest mentality possible. He would never be able to give up. She knew how tough things were in the real world—she was living it.

But things took a turn for the worse for the family in 1988. Freeman was injured in an accident and was unable to work. The family's finances began to suffer more.

Just when it looked as if things could not get worse for the family, Allen's youngest sister, Liesha, began suffering seizures. Doctors could not diagnose the problem right away and lots of expensive medical tests had to be performed before her condition could be identified and treated. The family could not afford the tests and was seriously in debt. They owed lots of money.

That's when Michael Freeman, Allen's stepfather, made a critical mistake. He thought he could help the family's money problems by selling drugs. He was convicted of trying to sell drugs and was

*Iverson smiles as he walks off the court at the end of a playoff game.*

sent to prison. Allen was devastated. The only male role model he ever had was a drug dealer. The angry young man became even angrier.

Allen started blaming his family's situation on Freeman. It would take years before he could forgive his stepfather and even try to understand why he did the things he did.

"He never robbed anybody," Iverson later said. "He was just trying to feed his family. It would kill him to come home from jail and find out how his family was living. One time he came home and just sat down and cried."[2]

While Freeman was in jail, Allen sometimes had to stay home from school to babysit his sister, Liesha. It was during those dark days that Allen created a plan in his head to never give up on basketball or football. One or the other was going to be his ticket out of poverty.

So when Allen attended Bethel High School he put all of his energy into playing sports. Sometimes he had run-ins with teachers over attendance and his poor attitude. Other teachers understood just how hard Allen had it and were more understanding.

Allen starred in football and basketball at the school and would eventually be named the state's high school football player and basketball player of the year by the Associated Press.

But things were not always good between Allen and his mother. In fact, when he was 16 the two just were not getting along at all, and Iverson was lucky enough to be invited to live with his former elementary school basketball coach, John Moore. It was in Moore's care that Allen learned the importance of discipline and the importance of doing well in school.

He was held to a strict style of life that Allen needed at the time. He would wake up at the same time every day, attend school, and be on time for everything he was supposed to do. But Allen wanted to work things out with his mother. He missed her and his little sisters. After a year he wanted to go back home.

> "They taught me to set goals so I could realize my dreams. That was the best thing I could have had."
>
> —Ann Iverson

Ann kept trying as well. She started working selling Amway, and she admits that it helped her focus on the important things in life.

"They taught me to set goals so I could realize my dreams," she said. "That was the best thing I could have had. Because all I had in the 'hood was people telling me how to sell drugs."[3]

*Iverson goes through his freethrow drills before a game in March 2003.*

His mother did not sell drugs and tried her best to provide the type of environment that Allen could thrive in, but there was no escaping the ghetto, along with its violence and crime. When he was fourteen years old, Allen's best friend was stabbed to death. Another time, Allen was at a party at a hotel in Hampton when there was an argument that ended up with guns being drawn. It certainly was not the typical childhood enjoyed by others his age growing up in nice neighborhoods. No, for Allen Iverson, things always seemed a little harder, except on the basketball court where, despite his average height, he was better than all the rest.

Allen never took drugs and never played with weapons, but it was all around him, all the time. He would soon learn that just being in the wrong place at the wrong time could land him in a heap of trouble. It would be the lesson of a lifetime.

# 3

# WRONG PLACE, WRONG TIME

We have all heard the expression "being in the wrong place at the wrong time." Whenever something bad happens to someone that was seemingly out of their control, they always wonder what might have been if they had done something differently. Allen Iverson is no different.

At Bethel High School in Hampton, Virginia, Allen was like many other high school students living in an urban environment. Except for one major difference: Allen was a top athlete, starring in basketball and football. He was an average student, but as long as he stayed out of trouble he was sure to earn some sort of college scholarship and become the first member in his mother's family to attend school beyond the twelfth grade.

Most people, Allen included, figured he would don a helmet and outrun people on the gridiron playing football.

"I always figured I was going to go to one of those big football schools, Florida State, Notre Dame," Allen said. "Football was my first love. It still is. I was going to go to one of those schools and play both. I just loved running the option, faking, throwing the ball, everything about football. I didn't even want to play basketball at first. My mother's the one who made me go to tryouts. I thank her forever."[1]

Yes, Allen was on his way to a big-name college with a big-time athletic department. All he had to do was keep playing sports and stay out of trouble.

But the young man, who seemingly had overcome terrible poverty and was about to earn himself an education, was about to see his life change forever. The fateful night started on February 13, 1993, when Allen and his friends decided to go bowling. It would be a nice quiet night with friends away from the neighborhood. Allen was a senior in high school and well-known as the local high school superstar.

Allen was with several friends, all African

American, and they had already bowled a few games when Allen and a friend decided to visit the snack bar. To get to the food counter, Allen and his friend had to walk by a group of white teenagers and young men from the neighboring town of Poquoson. Words were exchanged and Allen would later say that they were using racial slurs against them.

There are many accounts of what happened next. One of the white men, twenty-three-year-old Steve Forrest, said that Iverson's friend punched him in the head. Another eyewitness said that one of the white kids started it by throwing a chair. No matter what the details were of the fight's origin, soon it became an all-out brawl. People came running from both ends of the bowling alley. They met in the middle in what turned out to be an ugly episode.

> "I always figured I was going to go to one of those big football schools, Florida State, Notre Dame. Football was my first love."
>
> —Allen Iverson

Allen said he had left immediately, though some disputed his claims. Regardless, a few days later, Allen was one of four youths arrested for the incident—all African American. Charges of bias started up. Soon the case took on even uglier racial overtones as the state decided to try Allen, only seventeen, as an adult.

Allen's attorney at the time decided it would be best to skip a jury trial and simply have a judge hear and try the case. Iverson was found guilty and sentenced to fifteen years in prison. That's when the case started drawing national attention. Reporters from national magazines and television stations went to Hampton and started writing about the town. It became a political powder keg that would finally wind up with Virginia Governor Douglass Wilder.

Meanwhile, with the media documenting Allen's tragedy and the seeming end to his sports career, the seventeen-year-old prisoner did not allow his new circumstances to deter him from his goals, from his dreams of one day being able to lift his mother and sisters out of poverty. Allen knew that if he still had any chance of attending college and playing either basketball or football, he would need a high school diploma. Obviously, stuck behind bars, he was unable to attend his high school. But Allen studied hard and was determined to earn his equivalency diploma.

He also practiced basketball every single night, shooting baskets through a makeshift broken hoop

Allen Iverson had to overcome great adversity growing up before finally finding success as an NBA superstar.

nailed to a wall. He did not let the situation or the conditions stop him. Allen was on a mission.

"I had a bigger picture for my life," he said. "I wasn't [going] back to the sewer."[2]

Still, Allen hated reading about himself in the local newspapers as he served his sentence at the Newport News City Farm. He cried himself to sleep at night. But Allen decided to use the words that he read about himself to make himself stronger. He decided to make them a motivational tool, to push himself even harder than he already had.

> "I had a bigger picture for my life. I wasn't [going] back to the sewer."
>
> —Allen Iverson

Allen's high school principal, his mother, and even those who never met him decided to flood Governor Wilder's office with phone calls and letters asking him to intervene on Allen's behalf. Four months after he was jailed, Allen was released when his term was reduced.

However, the hard work was not coming to an end. While he sat in prison, Allen worked with a personal tutor, Sue Lambiotte, who agreed to help Allen earn his high school degree for no payment. She was very hard on Allen and would accept nothing less than his best effort. She accepted no excuses for missed homework assignments, for being late, for not completing his work in class, or any other infraction.

Lambiotte had known Allen for several years. Her youngest son, Clay, once played with Allen during a summer basketball league. She remembered him as being the team clown, the one who would amaze teammates with impersonations or drawings of his favorite basketball players. But she also knew that there was more to Allen than clowning around. She remembered him as a smart kid who maybe just needed a push into schoolwork.

One of the conditions of Allen's release was that he had to continue the tutoring sessions. One of the worst parts of this, for Allen, was that her learning center was located in Poquoson, Virginia, the same neighborhood where some of the white teenagers involved in the bowling alley fight lived.

"There was a lot of tension for Allen driving into that town," Lambiotte said. "But he kept coming."[3]

Allen stayed out of trouble and concentrated on his studies. Then on September 2, 1994, Allen passed his final exam. Lambiotte held a private graduation ceremony for Allen. He had done it. Allen was a high school graduate.

Now, the next obstacle Allen would face was trying to find a school anywhere that was interested in him. Before the bowling alley incident just about every major college basketball and football program in the country was interested in giving Allen a full sports scholarship to attend their school. Now, Allen could not find one. Despite his claims of innocence, Allen was seen as a troublemaker, and schools were no longer interested. It would take some major convincing on Allen's part to get any schools to even consider him. It would also be difficult to prove that he was still the gifted athlete he was as a high school junior. Because of the bowling alley incident and the time spent in prison, Allen was unable to play school sports as a senior. In reality, he had taken a full year off from sports.

No one would touch him. It appeared as if Allen would have to attend a junior college first and work his way back into the good graces of the major colleges. He would probably need to prove that he could stay out of trouble before a scholarship would come his way.

But finally Allen would have a stroke of good fortune. One coach called. It was legendary college basketball coach John Thompson of Georgetown University, near the nation's capital. Georgetown has long been known as a college basketball powerhouse, consistently competing in the NCAA Tournament

*Head Coach John Thompson helped Allen Iverson grow a great deal as both a player and a person while Iverson was at Georgetown.*

as well as turning out such National Basketball Association superstars as Patrick Ewing, Alonzo Mourning, and Dikembe Mutombo.

After Georgetown expressed interest, a few other top-notch basketball programs started calling as well. They were afraid that Allen would go to a competing school and beat them in a big game.

But Allen chose Georgetown.

More important, however, was the fact that Coach Thompson was regarded in the basketball

*Dikembe Mutombo (above) was a star player at Georgetown before making it big in the pros. Mutombo would later play alongside Allen Iverson with the Philadelphia 76ers.*

world as a coach that accepted no nonsense or disrespect from his players. He ran a tight ship and expected everyone to pay attention to his rules or else they would no longer be welcome on the team. It was just the kind of rigorous discipline that Allen needed.

At first, Allen was very surprised that none of the big college football schools called him at all.

"When the trouble came, it seemed the basketball people were the ones who stayed interested," he said. "I went to Georgetown because it was the best thing for me to do at the time, just play basketball. They didn't have any football, at least none that I wanted to play."[4]

A few months after being released from prison and a short time after celebrating his high school graduation alone with his tutor, Allen was ready to leave the ghettos and settle in at Georgetown. He knew a college education and a chance to play basketball at the highest amateur level in the United States would give him a chance to raise his family up from the poverty they had always known. Yet, when Allen's mother and sister dropped him off at the prestigious Catholic university, he cried at the thought of being so far away from them.

# 4

# HOYA OH-BOYA!

Allen Iverson looked like a little kid playing a big man's game as he donned the baggy silver and black No. 3 Georgetown Hoya uniform before a game against the Boston College Eagles—a Big East Georgetown rival. The Big East is the name of the conference where the Hoyas, the Eagles, and other schools like St. John's and Seton Hall compete.

Allen Iverson was wide-eyed and anxious, but not nervous, as his eyes darted around the court and the stands while Coach John Thompson tried hard to get his message across to his young player—the most talked-about college freshman in a long time.

Iverson tried to listen to the coach that saved his

basketball career and hopes for a college education, but he was having a hard time ignoring the crowd.

They yelled things like "Jailbird," or "Go back to jail, Iverson." Iverson pretended not to hear them, but he did, and the words stung him.

Despite having his name cleared, earning a high school diploma, and being accepted into one of the best college basketball programs in the country, Iverson still faced a great deal of work. There were still many obstacles that he had clear before he could succeed.

But Iverson, thanks in part to Coach Thompson's coaching and advice, used the pain from the words to make his game even tougher. In fact, the two men were immediately drawn together and formed a tight bond. Thompson became the father figure that Iverson so desperately needed for much of his young life. Like many of the players who came before him— the majority from broken homes—Iverson had started calling his coach, "Dad."

Iverson's game is fearless, much like his own personality. He does not shy away from trying to dribble through double-teams, daring players to try and steal the ball as he dribbles it very high and back and forth through his legs. Iverson cannot change who he is. He is a tough guy and will continue to play like one. His effort and attitude paid off. As a rookie, Iverson quickly found himself leading the Hoyas in just about every important category from scoring to steals to assists. Unlike many young players, Iverson never let a poor first half have any effect on how he played the second half of the game.

In a game against Big East rival Seton Hall, Iverson was held scoreless in the first half of an important conference game. Seton Hall's stifling defense practically took Iverson out of the game by double-teaming him and putting pressure on the ball every time he touched it. It was a nip-and-tuck game, but the Hoyas held a two-point lead at halftime.

**Despite having his name cleared, earning a high school diploma, and being accepted into Georgetown, Iverson still faced a great deal of work.**

The second half was the time for Iverson to show the crowd of hecklers and Seton Hall players what all the hype was about. Early in the third quarter Iverson dribbled the ball several times through his legs before throwing up a three-pointer—swoosh! Then he raced back downcourt at full speed to steal a pass. He dribbled the ball back downcourt, faked a jump shot, and then rifled a bullet of a pass to a streaking teammate for an easy

*Allen Iverson drives past Jason Martin of Texas Tech during an NCAA tournament game in March 1996.*

backdoor lay-up. It was a tremendous display of both offense and defense—total basketball.

After that particular game, reporters crowded around Iverson's locker to talk to him. Unfortunately, not many wanted to know about his crossover dribble, the halftime adjustments he had made, or how he single-handedly took apart Seton Hall's defense. No, the majority of reporters wanted to keep hearing about the bowling alley incident.

Iverson answered the questions wearily and patiently. He had truly bought into Coach Thompson's tough, no-nonsense style of coaching. Thompson stresses a "whole-person" program for his players. The "whole-person" program is simple. Thompson does not expect his players to work hard only on the basketball court. He expects players to behave courteously, to excel in classes, to treat people with respect, and to never stop working hard—at life. To top it off, Thompson is never just a basketball coach. He becomes a mentor, a friend, and sometimes a "Dad."

"I wasn't a Georgetown fan as a kid," Iverson said, "but I was a John Thompson fan."[1]

As a freshman Iverson was thrust immediately into the team's starting lineup—a rarity for as kid just out of high school who did not even play basketball as a senior. Inserted as the team's starting point guard, Iverson was up to the challenge. He was named Big East Player of the week several times and was the primary reason why the Georgetown Hoyas were nationally ranked, especially with senior guard George Butler removed from the team for poor grades. For the most part, Iverson was asked to carry the team—a tall order for a not-so-very-tall nineteen-year-old.

That's not to say Iverson did not experience growing pains in school. His play was sometimes erratic and out of control. He also sometimes was accused of shooting first and looking to pass second, not a great trait for a point guard. Because Iverson was clearly the most talented scorer on the team, it made sense for him to look for the open shot. But like other good players, Iverson knew where he needed to improve: patience. "My coach tells me all the time and I know that I need that more than any-thing," Iverson said.[2]

Iverson, despite his rough exterior and in-your-face demeanor on the court, was able to recognize how important it was to have the stabilizing pres-ence of Coach Thompson in his life.

"Coach Thompson was like a father figure to me, right off hand, it just clicked," Iverson said after his

*Allen Iverson (far left) has a conversation with three of his Georgetown teammates, Aw Boubacar, Jerome Williams, and Jahidi White (left to right) during a break in a game.*

freshman season at Georgetown. "Ninety percent of having a relationship with him is things that occur off-court. He helped me through last year. I didn't want to come here and just do anything. Any problems that I have I can just go to him and he'll sit down and listen. It's a lot more than player-coach between us. I don't think I could have made it through last year without him."[3]

Whatever it was, a combination of hard work, natural basketball skills, and a relationship with a coach who really cared about Iverson, it sure worked. He wowed the college basketball world by consistently proving that he was one of the quickest basketball players of all time—on any level. His lightning speed caught everyone's eye. He was named the Big East Rookie of the Year and Big East Defensive Player of the Year. University of Arkansas basketball coach Nolan Richardson said that he had never seen anything like Allen's speed on the basketball court. That was quite a compliment because as a long-standing fixture at Arkansas, Richardson has seen some of the fastest basketball players to move from the college ranks to the pros.

Iverson played 30 games in his first season at Georgetown. He averaged 20.4 points per game as well as 4.5 assists per game.

There was some talk after his freshman year that Iverson might forego his final three years of college and enter the NBA draft. But he still knew that he had work to do and that his game needed to get better in order to advance to the next level. He also needed to get stronger. Playing in the National Basketball Association is a lot different than playing in college. In the NBA, the players are faster, bigger, and much stronger.

Iverson worked hard at getting stronger during the summer between his freshman and sophomore seasons at Georgetown. He wanted to come back

*Iverson slam dunks the ball against Mississippi Valley State on March 15, 1996.*

for his sophomore season as a more controlled and complete player than he was as a freshman. That summer he was even lucky enough to participate in several basketball games that featured NBA players. The games were wide open with lots of scoring, and Iverson did not shy away from playing with guys that had professional experience. He even scored 70 points in a game a few times.

When Iverson decided to play at least one more year at Georgetown, it was a very tough decision. It was not easy for him to refuse the millions of dollars that were waiting for him in the NBA to keep attending college classes. Iverson, who had been poor his entire life, desperately wanted to help his family. He knew all too well how they were suffering.

"Every time I came home, it seemed like their living situation got worse," Iverson said of his mother and sisters.[4]

If Iverson impressed the basketball world with his play as a freshman, then his play as a sophomore was simply the icing on the cake. As a sophomore, Iverson still played the game with reckless abandon, but learned how to minimize the mistakes. Some onlookers were surprised that Coach Thompson— who was long known for his slow, plodding offensive

*Iverson hoists up his arms victoriously after his Georgetown Hoyas win a big NCAA tournament game in March 1996.*

strategies, allowed Iverson to play so wildly on the court.

Thompson responded by saying that the last thing Iverson needed was structure on the basketball court. He said that Iverson needed to be free, like a bird, to be able to see all of his dreams come true.

That season, Iverson led the Georgetown Hoyas to within one game of reaching the prestigious Final Four in the 1995–96 season. He averaged 25 points per game and was named a First Team All-American by the Associated Press, a very prestigious honor. Proving that he was more than just an incredible scorer, Iverson was also once again named the Big East Defensive Player of the Year.

> "I wasn't a Georgetown fan as a kid, but I was a John Thompson fan."
>
> —Allen Iverson

No athlete who ever played for Coach Thompson at Georgetown had ever left school to become a professional basketball player before graduating. Thompson was always able to convince his players that staying in school was more beneficial to them in the long run. But Coach Thompson knew that Iverson's case was different. He knew how bad the situation was for Iverson's mother and his two sisters. He also knew that Iverson now had a daughter of his own, Tiaura, and a girlfriend, Tawanne Turner, that he needed to take care of. This was the first time that Thompson thought it would be better if one of his players left school early, claiming hardship and applying for the NBA draft.

Thompson introduced Iverson to a sports agent named David Falk, and the three men devised a strategy. It was clear that Iverson would be one of the top players chosen in the June NBA draft. It was time.

Allen Iverson was ready for the NBA.

# NBA

Several great college basketball players were eligible for the 1996 NBA draft. In addition to Allen Iverson, there was point guard Stephon Marbury, power forward Marcus Camby, and guards Shareef Abdur-Raheem and Ray Allen. There was also a high school kid who had applied for the NBA draft by the name of Kobe Bryant.

But many of the basketball experts were already saying that the Philadelphia 76ers would be crazy if they did not select Iverson with the first pick of the draft. The previous year they had won only 18 games while losing 64. They were a team in dire straits.

Iverson, who never lacks confidence, visited only

one NBA city in the weeks before the draft: Philadelphia. He instantly fell in love with the city. There was so much to do and see, and he loved that there was an urban environment that he could relate to. Iverson was hoping that this was where he would end up.

While Iverson was impressed with the city, it was clear that the Philadelphia organization was impressed with him, too.

"He can dominate portions of the game," said Philadelphia General Manager Brad Greenburg after watching Iverson work out. "He's got the right stuff inside his heart, is a very hard worker, a tremendous talent and very competitive. I don't think it's a stretch to assume he's got a chance to be a great player in the NBA."[1]

The Philadelphia 76ers wasted little time once the draft started, and quickly announced Iverson as the number one player chosen. Iverson's lifelong battle with poverty was won. No longer would his mother, sisters, or girlfriend have to suffer or want. Iverson would rescue them all.

The day Iverson was drafted, Mayor James Easton of Iverson's hometown of Hampton announced he would hold a parade in Iverson's honor. It took only a few days after the draft for

Iverson to sign his name to a contract that would pay him almost $4 million a year. But even more impressive is that, despite never having played an NBA game, the Reebock sneaker company signed Iverson to a ten-year, $50 million deal to appear in their commercials. Bubba Chuck would never be poor again.

Iverson was definitely more suited for the wide-open NBA game than he was for the college style of play. He was able to be more creative, able to take more shots, able to go coast-to-coast with relative ease, and able to put up some big numbers. Of course, there were also some problems. As a point guard, Allen Iverson was sometimes too reckless and too careless with the ball, and often did not try to get his teammates involved in the flow of the game. There were lots of turnovers, too. It seemed that for every spectacular dunk or razzle-dazzle move there was also a bad decision or careless pass that resulted in an easy bucket for the opposing team.

> "He can dominate . . . He's got the right stuff inside his heart [and] is a very hard worker."
>
> —Brad Greenburg
> Philadelphia 76ers GM

Iverson's first game as a pro NBA player was an outstanding effort. Despite missing his first few

*Allen Iverson brings the ball upcourt against the Chicago Bulls during a game from his rookie season in 1997.*

shots badly and even having some blocked, he finally got himself on track and wound up with 30 points, 6 assists, and only 3 turnovers in 37 minutes played.

Over time it was clear that Iverson still had a lot to learn. Yet when he was good, he was truly spectacular. There was one game in particular when he was being guarded by the legendary Michael Jordan. Iverson broke him down so badly on one play that Jordan did not even have time to react. He simply turned around and watch Iverson go in for the slam dunk. Iverson was chosen to participate in the Schick NBA Rookie Game, which takes place during All-Star weekend. He scored 19 points and dished out 9 assists to earn the game's most valuable player award.

Iverson's great play, however, did not result in a better team just yet for Philadelphia. There were just too many holes, and despite having an outstanding scorer in Jerry Stackhouse, he and Iverson never seemed to be able to get into an offensive rhythm. As the season wound down and it was clear that Philadelphia would not be making the playoffs, Iverson started concentrating on his other goal. He wanted to win the league's rookie of the year award very badly. But he was seeing some very stiff competition, especially from Marbury, who had teamed up with wonder-child Kevin Garnett in Minnesota to make the Timberwolves one of the better and more exciting teams in the league.

While Iverson was getting a lot of attention for his scoring feats, Marbury was being noticed because his team was winning. But Iverson decided to make April his month. He played with reckless abandon and put up numbers that had never been seen before in the league. During one stretch, Iverson scored more than 40 points in five consecutive games. This was a new rookie record that eclipsed Hall-of-Famer Wilt Chamberlain's rookie record. Wilt the Stilt only did it in three games in a row his rookie season. In one of those five games, on April 12 against the Cleveland Cavaliers, Iverson actually poured in 50 points! The only other player in the league to even reach 50 points for the 1996–97 season was none other than Michael Jordan. Being mentioned in the same sentence with Chamberlain and Jordan certainly put Iverson up there with some of the all-time greats.

Iverson was named Rookie of the Month for April for his spectacular scoring exhibitions. But, even throughout his array of jump shots, crossover dribbles, and highlight reel slams, the 76ers lost all five games. For some reason Iverson received a lot of

Allen Iverson dunks the ball against the Los Angeles Clippers on February 25, 1997.

criticism for this. Even though he was obviously out there on the court playing his hardest and putting up some incredible numbers, his critics wanted more. Former NBA player and television commentator Charles Barkley even went as far as to call Iverson, "Me, myself and Iverson," a reference to what Barkley saw as selfish play.

But Iverson did not let the criticism bother him. He knew that he was playing his best. Philadelphia finished the season with a record of 22–60, only a slight improvement from the year before. But Iverson had a great individual season, averaging 23.5 points per game and 7.5 assists. He also led his team in steals, assists, and three-pointers.

Shortly after the season was over, Iverson became the first Philadelphia 76er in history to win the rookie of the year award. Iverson became very emotional when he was given the award and, in fact, turned and presented the award to his mother.

"Without her, none of this would have happened," Iverson said. "I wouldn't have been anywhere near playing in the NBA if not for my mom. She gave me the heart that I have. She made me believe since I was young that I could do anything that I wanted to do."[2]

There were a lot of exciting changes awaiting

*During his rookie season, Iverson ran up a string of five straight games where he scored more than 40 points, breaking a rookie record previously held by the legendary Wilt Chamberlain (above).*

Iverson in his second NBA season. The most significant change was that the team had replaced Johnny Dawkins with new head coach Larry Brown. He was a proven winner with a no-nonsense approach at both the college and professional levels. He had been coach of the Kansas Jayhawks in 1988 and led them to a national championship. The team had also traded away Jerry Stackhouse and acquired players Theo Ratliffe and Aaron McKie.

With Stackhouse gone, Iverson was moved from point guard to shooting guard. He would get more shots and be expected to score more. Iverson went on to have a spectacular season once again, averaging 22.0 points per game while improving his field goal percentage and most other parts of his game. He led the squad in points scored, three-pointers, assists, and steals. Incredibly, however, for the second straight season he was not named to the All-Star Game.

Philadelphia, for the second straight year with Iverson on the team, improved its record. The team finished with a 31–51 mark. Two years after winning only 18 games, the team set its sights on a playoff berth for the 1998–99 season.

But the next season never got on track for Philadelphia or the rest of the NBA teams. A labor dispute between the NBA players and owners resulted in the first two months of the basketball season being wiped out.

When the season finally did start, Iverson was raring to go. He was named player of the month after averaging 28.5 points per game—including 46 points in a loss to the Spurs.

Incredibly, Iverson's first contract with the Sixers was already coming to an end, so the team moved quickly to sign their superstar to a six-year, $71 million contract. It appeared he would be in Philadelphia for years to come.

The move by Coach Brown to move Iverson away from the point guard position worked, as Iverson put up numbers that he never had before. He was even challenging Los Angeles Laker superstar Shaquille O'Neal for the NBA scoring title. But more importantly, Philadelphia was finally involved in a real-life playoff race.

> "I wouldn't have been anywhere near playing in the NBA if not for my mom."
>
> —Allen Iverson

With a 27–20 record, the Sixers needed to beat the tough Toronto Raptors in Philly to earn a playoff berth. But Iverson and the hometown advantage, including the Philadelphia faithful, were too much for Vince Carter and the Raptors. Philadelphia won the game 103–96, meaning the Sixers had clinched a playoff spot. In each conference the teams with the eight best records qualify for the playoffs.

Although making the playoffs was the most important accomplishment for Iverson, there was one more battle on a personal level for Iverson to wage: the scoring title war with O'Neal. The player who averages the most points per game for the entire season wins the scoring title. In Iverson's last game, he scored 33 points in a victory over the Detroit Pistons. That gave him an average of 26.8 points per game. O'Neal finished averaging 26.3 points per game, meaning that Philadelphia not only had a playoff team, but also a scoring champion.

> The move by Coach Brown to move Iverson away from the point guard position worked, as Iverson put up numbers that he never had before.

Philadelphia's first opponent in the playoffs would be the gritty Orlando Magic. Orlando was heavily favored to win the series by the experts. But Iverson had never been on the playoff stage and he performed incredibly. In fact, Iverson dominated the series. In Philadelphia's three victories in the series, Iverson scored 30, 33, and 37 points, respectively.

He also had 10 steals in one of the games—a playoff record!

Philadelphia was moving ahead to the second round of the playoffs against Reggie Miller and the Indiana Pacers. The Pacers were just too much for the young Sixer ballclub and swept the series. Despite the setback, it had been a great season for Iverson and the Sixers, and it was clear that more great things were to come.

# 6

# CENTER STAGE

Allen Iverson continued to improve the next season and was named a starter for the Eastern Conference All-Star team. In the contest, Iverson was the high scorer with 26 points. With a scoring title under his belt, the All-Star performance helped solidify Iverson's reputation as being one of the best players in the National Basketball Association.

The Sixers continued to improve as well, and for the second straight year the team qualified for the playoffs. It was quite an accomplishment for Iverson, who after only four short years in the league was able to lead his team to playoff appearances in two of them.

Unfortunately for the Sixers, the 1999–2000 season ended much like the previous season. The team got out of the first round of the playoffs with an easy 3–1 victory over the Charlotte Hornets but then just could not get by the Indiana Pacers, who took the series four games to one.

Iverson averaged 28.4 points per game during the season, his highest point total to date. Iverson and his teammates vowed to work even harder during the off-season and make it even further in the playoffs the next season. Iverson also wanted to start exploring some of his other interests outside of basketball. Iverson created the Cross Over Foundation for underprivileged kids, and started up a yearly basketball tournament in his hometown, called the Allen Iverson Celebrity Summer Classic. The tournament raises money for the Boys & Girls Clubs of Greater Hampton Roads as well as for the American Heart Association.

Iverson knew how tough it was for him to grow up on some mean streets, and he wanted to encourage kids to keep away from drugs and other bad influences. Iverson also made several appearances in a Philadelphia summer league that puts on exhibition games for Philadelphia kids that are unable to afford to go and see a live 76ers game.

Then there was Iverson's music. Iverson was already looked to by the rap world as an icon and an idol when he decided to record a rap album of his own. He had always been seen as one of the leaders of what he called the "Hip Hop Nation." And in fact, his cornrows, or braided hair, were how many identified him and related to him in the hip-hop or rap world. Iverson has always tried to be himself even if it did not fit in with the expectations of the mainstream media or corporate America. In fact, despite being one of the game's true rising superstars, the only endorsement deal Iverson had was for Reebok sneakers. Some people even referred to him as Tupac with a jump shot, a reference to the late rapper Tupac Shakur.

> Iverson created the Cross Over Foundation for underprivileged kids, and started up a yearly basketball tournament in his hometown.

But much like everything Iverson had done before, the decision to record a musical album spawned much controversy when critics and fans heard some of the lyrics. Some of the songs contained words that were seen as offensive to gay people, women, and even African Americans. After meeting with NBA Commissioner David Stern,

Iverson agreed that some of the lyrics could be seen as offensive and decided to change some of the words before the album was sold in stores.

"If individuals of the gay community and women of the world are offended by any of the material in my upcoming album, let the record show that I wish to extend a profound apology," Iverson said. "If a kid thinks that I promote violence by the lyrics of my songs, then I beg them not to buy it or listen to it. I want kids to dream and to develop new dreams."[1]

> "I want kids to dream and to develop new dreams."
>
> —Allen Iverson

Allen Iverson was recognizing how powerful his voice was. With his cornrows, do-rag, and many tattoos, Iverson is one of the most high-profile and easily recognizable people in sports. Although many critics consider his appearance to be an attempt to project a "thug" image, this is not Iverson's intention. Many of his twenty-one tattoos, for example, are meant to pay homage to his friends back home in the projects, or deal with issues of loyalty and friendship.

Iverson was trying to record a musical message about what it was like to grow up on the streets and about the violence he had seen. Shortly after the rap-album controversy and bad press Iverson was receiving in the media, he seemed to concentrate even more on his game. For the first time, he seemed to be on the same page as his head coach, Larry Brown, with whom Iverson had several run-ins about coaching style and playing time.

Despite the success Iverson and the team had enjoyed for the previous few seasons, Iverson and Coach Brown had always shared a love-hate relationship. The two basketball geniuses did not often agree on things ranging from practice intensity to player rotations in games.

The team, led by Iverson's nearly 25 points per game, cleared a very difficult part of the early season, jumping out to a 10–0 start and posting the best record in the Eastern Conference. Another reason for the team's good start was that Iverson was starting to put more emphasis on the non-scoring parts of his game. He was no longer concerned with just putting the ball in the hole, but instead, concentrated on every aspect of basketball.

"He's giving up the ball a lot more now," Coach Brown said. "He's more comfortable with the players around him. He's defending better, rebounding better and practicing better. His overall game is the best since I've been here."[2]

Iverson also knew that at age twenty-five, it was

*Allen Iverson's left bicep shows some of his many tattoos.*

time to take things a little more seriously than in years past. He had two children now: daughter Tiaura and Allen II, whom he calls "Deuce." Iverson had even met with the team's owner, Pat Croce, to let him know just how seriously he would be taking things.

Indeed, after the CD controversy, Iverson and his teammates played some of the best basketball Philadelphia has ever seen. By mid-February the team had the NBA's best record and had the highest winning percentage the franchise has ever enjoyed. And Iverson was simply having some monster games. He poured in 54 points on January 6 against the Cleveland Cavaliers, a night when the Sixers notched their eighth straight road win. This came two days after Iverson scored 41 against the Seattle Supersonics. After the game, Cleveland Coach Randy Wittman said that there was just no stopping Iverson that night. In fact, he tried putting different players on Iverson and showing him all types of defensive looks. It did not matter. Two weeks later Iverson scored 51 in a duel against Toronto's Vince Carter, who had 39 of his own. As the season progressed it was obvious the Sixers were one of the league's dominant teams. That's when, during Iverson's fifth year of NBA stardom, fans and media truly began to appreciate how great he really was and still is.

After all, Iverson is only six feet tall, which by NBA standards is small. Writers were comparing him to Nate "Tiny" Archibald, a 6-foot 1-inch player from the 1970s and '80s who once led the league in scoring and assists in the same season.

Iverson was named to the All-Star team once again, and this time he led the East from an improbable deficit to defeat the Western Conference and win the game's Most Valuable Player award. A few days after the All-Star game, Philadelphia made a bold trade it hoped would help carry the team to the next level. They traded away popular players Theo Ratliffe and Toni Kukoc for Atlanta's dominating defensive center Dikembe Mutombo.

> "He's defending better, rebounding better and practicing better. His overall game is the best since I've been here."
>
> —Coach Larry Brown

The move paid immediate dividends. Iverson won his second scoring title by averaging 31.1 points per game, becoming the first player since Michael Jordan to average more than 30 points a game for an entire season. The team finished with a 56–26 record, good enough to earn home court advantage throughout the Eastern Conference Playoffs, where they finally were able to get past an aging Indiana Pacer squad in the first round.

The next two rounds of the playoffs featured enough exciting, heart-stopping basketball to fill one sports highlight show after another. First, Iverson squared off against Vince Carter and the Toronto Raptors in a seven-game series that Philadelphia squeezed out.

Then the Sixers defeated the Milwaukee Bucks, led by Ray Allen, in another grueling seven-game series. Iverson, who missed one playoff game due to injury, played the entire playoffs through a series of nagging and painful injuries to his arms, hands, and thigh. Amazingly enough he averaged 32.9 points per game in 22 playoff games!

The last obstacle between Iverson and his first-ever NBA championship was the powerful Los Angeles Lakers. Although Iverson's heroics gave the Sixers a Game 1 victory, Los Angeles was just too much for Philadelphia to handle.

Still, it had been a tremendous year for the Sixers, who not only made it all the way to the NBA Finals, but also became the first team in the history of basketball to boast four major awards. Iverson was named the league's Most Valuable Player, Coach

*Allen Iverson proudly holds up his 2000 All-Star Game MVP trophy.*

Brown was named Coach of the Year, Mutombo was named Defensive Player of the Year, and Aaron McKie was awarded the Sixth Man of the Year trophy.

Injuries really took their toll on the Sixers the following season. In fact, the team started out with Iverson, McKie, and point guard Eric Snow all on the sidelines nursing injuries. The team started out 0–5 and never seemed to get back on track, despite bursting through with some winning streaks, including a seven-game streak right after the 0–5 start in which Iverson was named Player of the Week. In January Iverson scored a career-high 58 points during an overtime win against the Houston Rockets. For his efforts, Iverson was once again named NBA Player of the Week. But Iverson got to play in only 60 games because of injuries, most notably a fractured hand suffered in Boston during a game in March. The team, however, pulled together and managed to snare its fourth straight playoff appearance by nabbing the sixth spot out of eight. The team squared off against a young and hungry Boston Celtic team, and they quickly fell behind two games to none. Iverson and the Sixers won the next two games before finally losing the series in Boston, a 120–87 defeat.

*Iverson drives past Antoine Walker of the Boston Celtics during an Eastern Conference playoff game in May 2002.*

But the team was proud of its accomplishments during what was an injury-riddled season. In fact, only three times during the season was the entire roster of players healthy and able to play.

Unfortunately, the following summer, Iverson once again found himself involved in controversy. Iverson was arrested for threatening two men with a gun after he had an apparent argument with his wife. Charges were later dropped and Iverson's name was cleared.

On the court, Iverson continued to battle nagging injuries, but the team, with a revamped lineup, continued to play well. The team was 28–24 in mid-February of the 2002–03 season and on its way to a fifth straight playoff appearance. Gone, however, was shot-blocking center Dikembe Mutombo, who had been traded to the New Jersey Nets for slashing forward Keith Van Horn. The Sixers hoped that Van Horn would provide enough scoring to keep some of the pressure off of Iverson.

As the 2003 playoffs began, it seemed as if this plan would work well. In the first round of the playoffs, with the Sixers facing the New Orleans Hornets, Iverson exploded for 55 points in the opening game. This was a Sixers playoff record! However, in the next four games of the series,

*Allen Iverson's shot is contested by the Milwaukee Bucks' Glenn Robinson during Game 6 of the 2001 Eastern Conference Finals. In July 2003, Robinson would join Iverson as a teammate in Philadelphia as a result of a four-team trade.*

Iverson's shooting hand went cold, as he made just 41 out of 109 shots. Philadelphia wound up splitting these four games, which left them with a 3–2 series edge. Game 5 was a particularly disappointing loss though, since it came on the Sixers home floor in Philadelphia, where the team could have wrapped up the series.

But Iverson and his teammates showed their true character and poise when they came back to win Game 6, on the road in New Orleans, to eliminate the Hornets four games to two. Iverson regained his form in the game, finishing with 45 points, including a pair of clutch baskets in the game's final two minutes. His last shot was one for the highlight reel. After momentarily losing control of the dribble, Iverson slipped free of defender Baron Davis with a head fake and then, with ten seconds left, launched a straightaway jumper that went in off the glass.

"That shot Iverson hit at the end was a miraculous shot—a bank shot from dead on," said Hornets Head Coach Paul Silas. "A big-time player stepped up."[3]

"This was a war," Iverson later said of the game—the tenth playoff game of 40 or more points in his career. "This reminded me of the wars back with the Indiana Pacers when we couldn't beat them, and then when we were finally able to beat them, it was still a war. We still had to fight."[4]

Unfortunately, Philly was then eliminated in the Eastern Conference Semifinals by the Detroit Pistons in six games. The Sixers lost the deciding sixth game in overtime despite Allen Iverson's 38 points and 9 assists. It was a disappointing, early end to the season for the Philadelphia 76ers.

As the offseason began, big changes were afoot for the team. First, Coach Brown left the team to take over as the new head coach of the Detroit Pistons. Then in July, in a large trade involving four teams, the Sixers dealt Keith Van Horn and got back Glenn "Big Dog" Robinson in return. In Robinson, Philly fans believed they had finally acquired the second big scorer they needed to take some of the pressure off of Allen Iverson. Like Iverson, Robinson had been a number one draft pick. Robinson also had averaged more than 20 points a game over the course of his nine-year career and was a two-time all-star. Iverson was very happy to have him as a teammate.

> "That shot Iverson hit at the end was a miraculous shot . . . . A big-time player stepped up."
>
> —Head Coach Paul Silas

"Glenn is just a better player than all those other guys who have been here," Iverson said. "It's as simple as that."[5]

"Iverson has been doing his thing here for a long time, and that's not going to change," Robinson added. "I'm just here to make it easier for him."[6]

When the 2003–04 season began, it appeared as though the pairing of Iverson and Robinson might surpass expectations. In an early game against the Chicago Bulls, the Sixers won in a blowout, 106–85. At one point, Iverson made a brilliant play, finding Robinson open behind the three-point line—a shot Robinson made easily.

"I noticed during the game he was in the corner and I penetrated to the basket and his man helped, and just for that second he was open and hit a three," Iverson said. "I think Glenn makes the game so much easier for me. Guys got to play me honest now."[7]

Unfortunately, shortly after the Chicago game, Robinson would suffer a sprained left ankle, putting him on the shelf for awhile. Iverson would do his best to carry the team while Robinson was out. Against the Atlanta Hawks on November 29, he poured in 50 points in leading the Sixers to a 98–86 victory. It was the ninth time in his career, including the playoffs, that Iverson scored 50 or more points in a game.

To fans of Number 3, Allen Iverson, it does not matter much who the other four players on the court are. They know that Iverson, "The Answer," will be out there playing his hardest and doing what he does best: putting the basketball through the hoop.

# CHAPTER NOTES

### Chapter 1. Greatest Game

1. Associated Press, "Perfect No More," June 6, 2001, <http://sportsillustrated.cnn.com/basketball/nba/2001/playoffs/news/2001/06/06/sixers_lakers_ap> (September 15, 2003).
2. Ibid.
3. Leigh Motville, "Flash Point," *Sports Illustrated*, December 9, 1996, p. 63.

### Chapter 2. Bubba Chuck

1. Gary Smith, "Mama's Boys," *Sports Illustrated*, April 23, 2001, <http://sportsillustrated.cnn.com/si_online/news/2002/05/08iverson_flashback/index.html> (September 15, 2003).
2. Rick Reilly, "Counterpoint," *Sports Illustrated*, March 9, 1998, p. 90.
3. Smith, "Mama's Boys."

### Chapter 3. Wrong Place, Wrong Time

1. Leigh Montville, "Flash Point," *Sports Illustrated*, December 9, 1996, p. 64.
2. Rick Reilly, "Counter Point," *Sports Illustrated*, March 9, 1998, p. 91.
3. Ibid., p. 92.
4. Montville, p. 64.

## Chapter 4. Hoya Oh-Boya!

1. David Falkner, "The Agony and the Ecstasy," *The Sporting News*, January 30, 1995, p. 32.
2. Ibid.
3. Iverson interview, <http://members.fortunecity. de/stefnba/iverson/georgetown.htm> (September 15, 2003).
4. Rick Reilly, "Counter Point," *Sports Illustrated*, March 9, 1998, p. 92.

## Chapter 5. NBA

1. Ernie Long, "Mr. Iverson Wants to Come and Play in Philadelphia," June 1998, <www.allen.iverson. net/articles/9697/want-to-be-in-philly.html> (September 15, 2003).
2. Don Bostrom, "Iverson Wins His Award for His Mom," June 1997, <www.allen.iverson. net/articles/9697/roy-for-his-mom.html> (September 15, 2003).

## Chapter 6. Center Stage

1. Julia Wood, "Iverson's Lyrics on Debut Album Ignites Controversy in NBA," *The Hoya*, October 13, 2000.
2. Associated Press, "Hungry: Same Old Iverson? Look Again," November 11, 2000, <http:// sportsillustrated.cnn.com/basketball/nba/news/ 2000/11/11/Iverson_ap/> (September 15, 2003).
3. "Iverson's 45 Sparks Sixers into Semifinals," NBA.com: Playoffs 2003, May 2, 2003, <http:// www.nba.com/games/20030502/PHINOH/recap. html> (December 22, 2003).
4. Ibid.

5. John Smallwood, "This Big Dog Can Shoot," *Philadelphia Daily News*, October 1, 2003, <http://www.twincities.com/mld/dailynews/6903150.htm> (December 5, 2003).

6. Ibid.

7. Associated Press, "Allen Iverson Praises Glenn Robinson After Sixers Dump Bulls 106–95," *Yahoo! Sports*, November 8, 2003, <http://ca.sports.yahoo.com/031108/6/vfau.html> (December 5, 2003).

# CAREER STATISTICS

## COLLEGE

| Season | Team | GP | FG% | REB | PTS | PPG |
|--------|------|-----|-----|-----|-----|-----|
| 1994–1995 | Georgetown | 30 | .390 | 99 | 134 | 20.4 |
| 1995–1996 | Georgetown | 37 | .480 | 141 | 173 | 25.0 |
| TOTALS | | 67 | .440 | 240 | 307 | 23.0 |

**GP**—Games Played
**FG%**—Field Goal Percentage

**REB**—Rebounds
**PTS**—Points
**PPG**—Points Per Game

# NBA

| Season | Team | GP | FG% | REB | AST | STL | BLK | PTS | PPG |
|--------|------|----|-----|-----|-----|-----|-----|-----|-----|
| 1996–1997 | Philadelphia | 76 | .416 | 312 | 567 | 157 | 24 | 1,787 | 23.5 |
| 1997–1998 | Philadelphia | 80 | .461 | 296 | 494 | 176 | 25 | 1,758 | 22.0 |
| 1998–1999 | Philadelphia | 48 | .412 | 236 | 223 | 110 | 7 | 1,284 | 26.8 |
| 1999–2000 | Philadelphia | 70 | .421 | 267 | 328 | 144 | 5 | 1,989 | 28.4 |
| 2000–2001 | Philadelphia | 71 | .420 | 273 | 325 | 178 | 20 | 2,207 | 31.1 |
| 2001–2002 | Philadelphia | 60 | .398 | 269 | 331 | 168 | 13 | 1,883 | 31.4 |
| 2002–2003 | Philadelphia | 82 | .414 | 344 | 454 | 225 | 13 | 2,262 | 27.6 |
| TOTALS | | 487 | .420 | 1,997 | 2,722 | 1,158 | 107 | 13,170 | 27.0 |

**GP**—Games Played
**FG%**—Field Goal Percentage
**REB**—Rebounds
**AST**—Assists
**STL**—Steals
**BLK**—Blocks
**PTS**—Points
**PPG**—Points Per Game

# WHERE TO WRITE

Mr. Allen Iverson
c/o The Philadelphia 76ers
First Union Center Complex
3601 S. Broad Street
Philadelphia, PA  19148

# INTERNET ADDRESSES

**NBA.com: Allen Iverson Bio**

http://www.nba.com/playerfile/allen_iverson/index.
html

**The Official Site of the Philadelphia 76ers**

http://www.nba.com/sixers

**Allen Iverson World**

http://www.alleniversonworld.com

# INDEX